JKJC

OCT 2022.

NEW YORK

Published in the United States by Del Rey, an imprint of Random House, a division of Penguin Random House LLC, New York.

DEL REY and the CIRCLE colophon are registered trademarks of Penguin Random House LLC.

Originally published in hardcover in the United Kingdom by Farshore, an imprint of HarperCollins Publishers Limited.

ISBN 978-0-593-15811-1
Ebook ISBN 978-0-593-15812-8

Printed in the United States on acid-free paper

randomhousebooks.com

2 4 6 8 9 7 5 3 1

First US Edition

Written by Thomas McBrien
Additional illustrations by Kate Bieriezjanczuk
Special thanks to Sherin Kwan, Alex Wiltshire and Milo Bengtsson

GUIDE TO SURVIVAL

CONTENTS

WELCOME TO THE *MINECRAFT: GUIDE TO SURVIVAL!*

There are many ways to play Minecraft, and one of the most popular is Survival mode. Here, you must find your own path through the game, crafting only with the blocks you can find and facing many dangers, knowing that with one false move, you might lose everything. It's super exciting – and super challenging!

Maybe you picked this book up because you're trying to survive your first night, or maybe you've started your journey and you're looking for a little support. Or maybe you're already an experienced hero and want to know what's in store for you on the other side of that mountain.

No matter your experience, this guide will introduce everything you need to know to set forth and succeed in Survival mode. You'll learn how to understand Minecraft's user interface and how to craft essential tools. Also, how to defend yourself against fearsome mobs and keep yourself well fed, and how to meet friendly villagers, brew potions and enchant your gear.

Finally, we'll set out for the weird and threatening dimensions of the Nether and the End, where you'll need to use everything you've learned to become the hero you were destined to be.

The world is big and full of adventure.

SO LET'S GET OUT THERE!

GETTING STARTED

BEDROCK EDITION & JAVA EDITION

Minecraft is available in two editions: Bedrock Edition and Java Edition. Both offer the same Minecraft experience, with only minor differences, but multiplayer is limited to each edition.

JAVA EDITION

BEDROCK EDITION

WHICH DEVICE?

You can play Minecraft on lots of devices, from cellphones to gaming consoles and even VR headsets. Depending on the device you use, you'll play either Bedrock Edition or Java Edition. Bedrock is the edition that allows cross-platform play between consoles, mobile devices and Windows, while Java is the original Minecraft edition and allows for cross-platform play between Windows, Linux and macOS.

TOP TIP

If you're unsure which edition to pick, ask your friends which they play. Using the same edition allows for cross-platform multiplayer!

Edit Server Info

Server Name

Minecraft Server _

Server Address

Server Resource Packs: Prompt

Done

Cancel

JOIN A SERVER

Looking to join your friends on an existing server? You can click on Multiplayer and join them by adding their server. Simply type in the server name and address, click Done and select the server from the Multiplayer menu.

Before you dive into the Overworld, you must first decide how you're going to play and on what device. If you want to play with your friends, it's important you choose the right game edition. This book focuses on Minecraft: Bedrock Edition, which differs ever so slightly from Minecraft: Java Edition.

SINGLE PLAYER VS. MULTIPLAYER

Once you've chosen an edition and installed the game, it's time to choose your adventure. In Minecraft you can choose to play either single player or multiplayer.

Multiplayer can be played online and in LAN mode (multiple devices in the same home). If you want to play with friends, you can join a LAN game on your network at home, or a server hosted online.

Single player is the default mode. If this is your first time playing, you should play in single player until you get used to the controls and the game. You may even find you prefer building and exploring alone!

SURVIVAL MODE

With unfamiliar terrain and dangerous mobs lurking nearby, taking your first step into the Overworld in Survival mode can be challenging. To get through it, you'll have to prepare yourself for the unknown dangers ahead. But where to start? With no set route to follow, it's up to you to forge your own path through this wild, blocky world. Read on to learn about Survival mode and staying alive in Minecraft. Let's get started!

WHAT IS SURVIVAL MODE?

WHY PLAY SURVIVAL MODE?

1 EXPLORE
Survival mode pits you against the elements. You can roam the land to uncover the secrets around you, but watch out for cliff edges, lakes of lava and many other natural dangers.

2 BATTLE MOBS
Explosive creepers and bow-wielding skeletons patrol for unsuspecting players to terrorize. Be prepared to face down – or run from – these mobs and ensure you live another day.

3 RESOURCES
You'll have to find and gather all the resources you need. While some will be easy to find, others will see you embark on daring adventures to faraway places.

4 SURVIVE
Hostile mobs spawn every nightfall, so it's up to you to plan ahead and ensure your survival by crafting equipment and building structures.

In Survival mode, players must explore, build and battle to survive. Starting with nothing but your wits to keep you safe, you must act quickly and gather resources to survive your first night and many more to come. Watch your step! There are many dangers to look out for.

RISK & REWARD

Survival mode is filled with the thrill of danger. Unlike in Creative mode, you will die if you run out of health points. Of course, you can always respawn, but you'll lose all your items and experience points. The added danger makes the game so much more rewarding.

DAY CYCLE

In Minecraft, time passes exactly 72 times faster than in the real world – that's a full day every 20 minutes. A complete day cycle will see the sun rise and fall. Keep an eye on the clock, for once the sun starts to set, a great number of mobs will start to spawn in dark corners, and seeing dangers becomes difficult in the low light. This is the most dangerous time in the game, not to mention, nothing grows in the dark so you're better off sleeping through it somewhere safe!

NIGHTTIME CLOCK

DAYTIME CLOCK

TOP TIP

Once it's dark you can sleep through the night by using a bed.

CUSTOMIZE YOUR NEW WORLD

GAME MODE

To get the most from this book, play in Survival mode. Creative mode gives you unlimited access to all the blocks and items available, while in Survival mode, it's up to you to gather resources to build, craft and survive. Java Edition players can also play Hardcore mode where the difficulty is set to Hard and you won't respawn if you die.

DIFFICULTY

There are three difficulty levels besides Normal: Peaceful, Easy and Hard. In Peaceful, players regain health rapidly and most hostile mobs don't spawn – those that do can't do damage. In Easy, mobs deal less damage, spawn with less equipment and cause less havoc. In Hard, mobs deal a lot more damage, and many spawn with powers that make them more dangerous.

ALLOW CHEATS

Toggle this option to allow cheats. Cheats will make your experience easier but will also prevent you from earning Advancements. Playing Survival mode is best played with cheats off.

DATA PACKS

Data packs allow you to customize your experience. These packs can change textures, create new Achievements and add and remove content. Find them on the Minecraft Marketplace.

GAME RULES

Here, you can toggle a number of default in-game options before generating your world. There are lots of settings you can change, such as increasing the tick speed or keeping your inventory after deaths.

When you first set up a new world, you will have the option to customize the world generation settings. These will define how your game is played, what the landscape will look like and how structures are generated. Depending on how you want to play, you can change these to best fit your needs.

SEED

Every world has a unique seed – a 19-digit identifier code used to generate a world. You can either generate a random seed or input an existing one to play in a world that generates with identical features for everyone using the same seed. This way you can replay favorite worlds or compare your Survival adventures with friends.

GENERATED STRUCTURES

Minecraft is full of generated structures (see pages 44 and 88). If you want to play in complete wilderness, you can toggle the Generated Structures option to stop them from popping up automatically. Progress in the game without them will be limited, though.

BONUS CHEST

Toggling this option will cause a chest to appear near the player's spawn point upon generating a new world. The chest contains a random collection of basic items for early game.

WORLD TYPE

Toggle this option to determine how worlds generate. The Default option will generate a varied, lush landscape, while the Superflat option will generate a flat grassland on Bedrock. Java players can create Amplified worlds with larger mountains and an unforgiving terrain.

PLAYER STATS

1 HEALTH BAR

These hearts represent your health bar. Each heart is worth two health points, and you can have a maximum of 20 health points. You lose hearts when you take damage, but they will regenerate when your hunger bar is full.

2 HUNGER BAR

Your hunger bar is made up of ten drumsticks, each worth two hunger points. It decreases when performing actions such as running, jumping and mining. A full hunger bar will regenerate health points.

3 EXPERIENCE BAR

Experience (XP) is obtained from experience orbs, received from actions such as mining, breeding, trading and defeating mobs. Gathering XP will raise your level, allowing you to enchant, etc., and is tracked on the green bar.

4 HOTBAR

The hotbar is a mini inventory for your most used items, weapons and tools on the HUD. You can toggle between these items without opening the inventory. It is good practice to keep your sword handy at all times.

TOP TIP

You can customize the blocks, tools and items that appear in your hotbar by accessing the inventory screen. The hotbar is the bottom row of the inventory screen, and you can move your owned items from the storage slots to your hotbar. Place useful things close together to easily switch between them.

It's time to step into the Overworld. Hit the "Play" button and create your first world. When you spawn, you'll be standing in a biome similar to this one. The heads-up display (HUD) shows you everything you need to know about your survival stats. Let's take a look at what it all means.

5 INVENTORY
Your inventory consists of 27 storage slots, an off-hand slot and a 2x2 crafting grid. Many blocks and items can be stacked together, to a maximum of 64, while others, such as tools, cannot be stacked.

6 OFF-HAND
You can equip a secondary item to your off-hand slot via your inventory. This allows you to dual-wield, though some players keep torches or shields in their off-hand slot, so that they can defend themselves.

7 ARMOR SLOTS
These are your equipment slots. You can wear a helmet, chestplate, leggings and boots to increase your defense and help you stay alive. Each piece of armor increases your total protection against attacks.

8 RECIPE BOOK
The recipe book is a catalog of recipes in Minecraft. It will show you everything you can create with the materials you have available in your inventory. Some recipes require a crafting table, though.

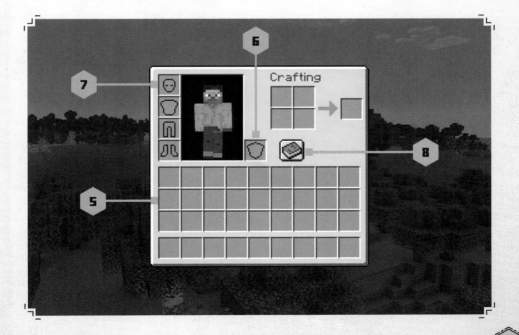

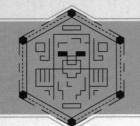

RESOURCES

BLOCKS

Blocks are basic units of structure that can be placed directly in the game world or used for crafting. You can collect blocks by punching, digging and mining with your fists or with crafted tools. Collecting, crafting and using blocks is essential to your survival.

Inventory

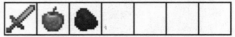

ITEMS

Items are objects that can be added to a player's inventory, such as food and crafting materials. Unlike blocks, items cannot be placed in the game world. They can be used in recipes and by your character.

TOOLS

There is a tool for every job in Minecraft. A lot of blocks can be collected by hand, but tools such as pickaxes and shovels will speed up the process. A flint and steel sets fire to some blocks, the compass helps you navigate and weapons aid you in battle (see page 18).

Look around the game and you'll see what Minecraft is made of: blocks. These blocks are your resources — use them to build, battle and survive. Some blocks and mobs drop items, and you can combine items and blocks to make tools. The more you play, the more you will discover!

USING RESOURCES

When you start a game, there will be trees that can be cut for wood, caves that can be plundered for coal and ores, and seeds that can be collected for crops. To really make the most of these resources, there are a couple of things you'll need to craft first, using your recipe book.

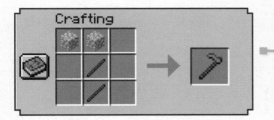

CRAFTING

You can craft in your inventory with four ingredients, but if you want to expand the range of your recipes, you can make a crafting table, which allows for nine ingredients. You can use your recipe book to figure out what to craft with the resources you have available.

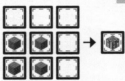

Crafting table recipe

TOP TIP

Many flammable resources can be used as fuel, such as coal and wood. You can also use wooden blocks, such as stairs and slabs.

Furnace recipe

FURNACES

The furnace can be used for cooking food and smelting blocks, allowing you to forge a multitude of useful items, such as iron ingots, glass and Nether brick. However, you must ensure it is kept fueled to continue smelting items.

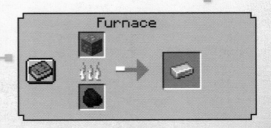

THE RIGHT TOOL FOR THE JOB

ATTACK STRENGTH & DURABILITY

Tools can be crafted out of wood, stone, iron, gold, diamond and netherite. The better the material used, the quicker you will collect resources and the longer your tool will last before it breaks. Better tools are also needed to collect rarer resources.

PICKAXE

TYPES						
ATTACK STRENGTH	1	3	4	2	5	6
DURABILITY	60	132	251	33	1562	2032

The pickaxe will likely be the first tool you craft in Minecraft and the one you use most. They are needed to mine ores, stones and metals. Specific pickaxes are needed to collect certain types of blocks – if you use a pickaxe that is too weak for the material you are collecting, the block will break and not drop anything.

AXE

TYPES						
ATTACK STRENGTH	3	4	5	3	6	7
DURABILITY	60	132	251	33	1562	2032

If you're looking to cut down trees or to quickly collect wood-based blocks, the axe is your go-to tool. However, the axe is a deadly weapon, too. Though slightly less powerful than the sword, you can use an axe to great effect when battling mobs.

SWORD

TYPES						
ATTACK STRENGTH	4	5	6	4	7	8
DURABILITY	60	132	251	33	1562	2032

The sword is your primary melee weapon. A good sword will come in handy when facing down dangerous mobs. Swords can also be used to mine certain resources, such as bamboo and cobwebs.

Whether you're growing food, chopping down trees or mining for diamonds, collecting resources is a large part of the game. As such, you will need the correct tools for the jobs – using an appropriate tool will increase your collection speed, while using the wrong one can destroy the block.

HOE

TYPES	🪓	🪓	🪓	🪓	🪓	🪓
ATTACK STRENGTH	2	3	4	2	5	6
DURABILITY	60	132	251	33	1562	2032

For players with green thumbs, the hoe is an invaluable companion. It is perfect for tilling dirt or grass blocks to create farmland and can also be used as a scythe to quickly harvest plant-based blocks.

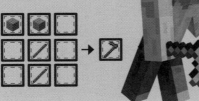

SHOVEL

TYPES	🥄	🥄	🥄	🥄	🥄	🥄
ATTACK STRENGTH	1	2	3	1	4	5
DURABILITY	60	132	251	33	1562	2032

Shovels are the quickest way to clear dirt, sand and other soft blocks. They can also turn dirt blocks into paths and extinguish campfires.

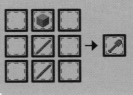

SHEARS

If you've got a sheep that needs trimming, the shears are the tool you need. They'll make light work of a sheep's coat and reward you with wool. They also have many other uses, such as harvesting seeds and cutting through cobwebs.

FLINT AND STEEL

A flint and steel is for sparking fires – use it to ignite extinguished campfires and candles, and to activate Nether portals. They're also useful for setting off TNT – but watch you don't blow yourself up by accident!

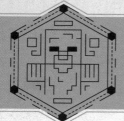

DIG A MINE

MINING TIPS

Mining is not just a game of chance – you can boost your yield of rare resources with these neat tricks.

LIGHTING

It's dark underground, so bring torches to light up the darkness and reveal what's around you. If you can't see the blocks, you won't know what you're mining! Light will also prevent hostile mobs from spawning.

LISTENING

Turn your volume up and listen carefully – do you hear the sound of dripping water or the groans of a nearby zombie? The noises you hear will tell you of nearby caverns and caves worth exploring. Or mobs worth avoiding!

TOP TIP

Turning on subtitles will help determine where noises are coming from.

LOCATION

If you're looking for specific blocks, it's important you're looking in the right places. While many blocks can be found throughout the game world, some can only be found in specific biomes. If you want to find gold ore, for instance, go find the badlands biome. Check out pages 38–45 to find out more about biomes.

Mining is an essential element of Survival gameplay. No matter what you're doing or where you're going, you will have to do some mining to progress in the game. Fortunately, mining is great fun and there are lots of ways to go about it, including tips for improving your yield.

HOW TO MINE

First, you must prepare. Before going on a mining expedition, make sure you have the resources to survive – a pickaxe, a shovel, torches and some food. Next, use an effective strategy to mine the maximum number of blocks with the least amount of digging.

BRANCH MINING

A popular mining strategy is branch mining. This is the easiest form of digging; simply grab your tools and start creating a hole in the ground. Making a series of passageways that branch out from a main route will allow you to cover a lot of ground.

PROS
- Can be done anywhere
- Lots of resources

CONS
- Hard to find specific resources
- It's a lot of work, so tools will be destroyed quickly

CAVING

Many players like to go caving. Simply explore the area around you and look for a cave opening leading underground. These caves will take you deep below the surface, and have lots of visible resources for you to pick.

PROS
- Tools last longer
- Resources are easier to find

CONS
- Can be hard to locate caves
- Easy to get lost
- Lurking mobs

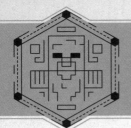

FOOD TIME

HUNGER

Your hunger level is as important as your health, because it can have an effect on your stats and abilities. A low hunger bar will make you slow on your feet. If it falls to zero, you'll start to lose health points and won't even be able to sleep.

20 HUNGER POINTS
Instantly regain two health points when you take damage.

6-17 HUNGER POINTS
You will neither lose nor gain health points.

6 HUNGER POINTS
You can no longer sprint.

18 HUNGER POINTS
You will slowly regenerate lost health points.

0 HUNGER POINTS
You will slowly lose health points.

Playing in Survival mode means keeping an eye on your health and hunger bars. If you let these fall too low, you'll soon find yourself struggling to stay alive! Every action you make will have an effect on your hunger bar, but thankfully you can replenish the bar by eating food.

Players have two food statistics: hunger and saturation. Both are increased by eating food, but only hunger is visible on the HUD. Saturation can decrease the need for eating as the higher your saturation level, the slower your hunger points will deplete. Among the best foods for saturation are melon slices, carrots – particularly golden ones – steak and porkchops. Your saturation level is set by the food you ate last, so be sure to eat well!

Naturally, you're going to want the best food to keep your hunger bar full. However, some foods can be difficult – and dangerous – to find. You'll get them eventually, but when you're starting out, you're better off focusing on easy-to-find foods. Why not try some of these tasty treats?

BEETROOT
With any luck, you'll come across some crops, such as beetroot, which you can then plant, grow and eat.

BREAD
You can craft bread using a crafting table and 3 wheat. Bread is a highly efficient and sustainable food source.

SWEET BERRIES
Sweet berries can be collected from sweet berry bushes, found in all taiga biomes. Watch out for the bush's sharp thorns!

BAKED POTATO
Baked potatoes are a filling food source. Cook potatoes in a furnace, a blast furnace or on a campfire.

RAW BEEF
Most farm animals drop raw meat. Cows will drop raw beef, which you can eat raw or cook for more hunger points.

BASIC FOOD

Most foods, such as fish, meat and fruit and vegetables, can be eaten alone and will simply replenish your saturation and hunger bar. Although the nutrition values may differ, you can always keep yourself fed with basic food items.

RECIPES

Some foods can't be eaten raw, or they offer little sustenance until they're crafted with other items in recipes. These crafted foods can be incredibly helpful, whether they're honey bottles for curing poison or a cake for your birthday party. Crafted recipes are generally much more nourishing, but they also require more resources. If you have a farm (see pages 26–29), you can use it to produce many of the ingredients you need. There are lots of tasty recipes to create, and you can find some of our favorites below.

Cake recipe

Golden apple recipe

Cookie recipe

As you explore, you're going to find more sources of food. Some can be eaten on their own and some can be crafted into delicious recipes. There are even foods with magical properties. Keep an eye out for edible items in the game, as having the right food in your inventory could save your life!

CURES & POISONS

Watch what you eat — and we're not talking about how many cookies you have before dinner! Some foods will hit you with a status effect, which can be beneficial or dangerous to your well-being. Rotten flesh will leave you poisoned while drinking milk will cure you of all status effects, even the good ones.

MAGICAL PROPERTIES

Some foods have magical properties, such as the chorus fruit. When you eat it, you might teleport randomly to a nearby location. This can be very helpful when falling, as it will teleport you safely to the ground and avoid fall damage.

EFFECTS

Learn about the effects you can receive from eating different foods.

ANTIDOTE	Cures Poison effect.	**POISON**	Inflicts damage over time.
ABSORPTION	Gain additional health hearts on your health bar.	**REGENERATION**	Restores the player's health over time.
BLINDNESS	Impairs the player's vision.	**RESISTANCE**	Reduces incoming damage.
FIRE RESISTANCE	Nullifies most fire-based damage.	**TELEPORT**	Teleport to a nearby block.
HUNGER	Causes hunger bar to deplete faster.	**WEAKNESS**	Decreases the player's attack power.
JUMP BOOST	Temporarily increases the player's jump height.	**WITHER**	Inflicts damage over time to the player.
NAUSEA	Warps and wobbles the player's vision.	**SATURATION**	Replenishes the player's hunger bar and reduces the need for eating.
NIGHT VISION	Enhances the player's ability to see in darkness and underwater.		

FARMING: CROPS

GROWING CROPS

Growing crops is the simplest way to gather food. There are several kinds of crops you can grow, from wheat and beetroot to carrots and potatoes. You can plant these either as seeds or as vegetables. Here are some useful ingredients for your crafted recipes.

BREAD

Wheat cannot be eaten as it's grown. However, placing 3 wheat in a crafting table will make a loaf of tasty bread.

CROP	GROW FROM	FOOD			
WHEAT	WHEAT SEEDS	5			
BEETROOT	BEETROOT SEEDS	1		6	
CARROT	CARROTS	3		6	
POTATO	POTATOES	1		5	
MELON	MELON SEEDS	2			
PUMPKIN	PUMPKIN SEEDS	8			

BEETROOT SOUP

Craft a bowl from wooden planks and add beetroots to craft some soup.

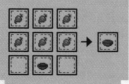

PUMPKIN PIE

If you have some chicken eggs and sugar, why not craft a pumpkin pie?

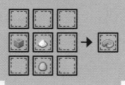

GOLDEN CARROT

Golden carrots can be eaten and used in crafting. Use 8 golden nuggets and a carrot to craft one.

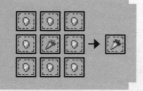

Food is essential for surviving in Minecraft, so you're going to want a steady supply to keep you nourished at all times. A farm is an excellent way to keep your kitchen cupboards full. You can farm either crops or mobs – or both! – and it's even possible to automate the process.

HOW TO PLANT CROPS

Before you can start growing your vegetables, you're going to need to prepare your farmland. Crops need three essential conditions to grow: farmland, water and light. This basic farm below has everything you need to start growing crops.

LIGHT

Crops need light to grow. The sun will grow your crops during the day, but you can also place light sources such as torches, so they continue to grow at night.

FARMLAND

To plant your seeds, you will need farmland. Simply use a hoe on some grass or dirt blocks to prepare the land. Once the land is prepared, plant any seeds you have in your inventory and watch them grow.

WATER SOURCE

Place a water source in your farmland by pouring a bucket of water. This keeps the soil irrigated and provides hydration to areas up to four blocks away from it.

HARVESTING CROPS

When your crops are fully grown, you can harvest the food by clicking on the crop. You can eat some of the crops raw, but others, such as wheat, will have to be crafted into delicious recipes.

TOP TIP

Did you know that bone meal will help grow your plants? Craft your bones into bone meal and use it on seeds to speed up their growth.

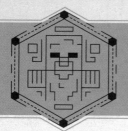

FARMING: MOBS

COLLECTING MEAT

In order to collect meat, you must first defeat the mob to make them drop their items. You can find mobs all across the Overworld, but the best strategy for maintaining your food supply is to create a farm and breed the mobs, or you will spend a lot of time searching for more when you run out.

TOP TIP

Defeating a mob with a Flame-enchanted bow or Fire Aspect-enchanted sword will cook the food items as they drop!

TOP TIP

Baby mobs do not drop items. Baby mobs take 20 minutes to grow into adults, or you can feed them to make them grow faster.

BREEDING MOBS

To breed mobs, you will need to find two of the same adult mob and feed them their favorite food. This will make them reproduce. Keep breeding mobs to produce more offspring until you have a thriving herd. Mobs can only be bred once every five minutes, so you'll need to be patient!

Farming mobs will provide you with a more nourishing source of food. However, it takes more work than farming crops. Before you can collect meat, you'll first need to breed your animals so that you don't run out of them. Farming mobs will also provide you with some useful items for crafting.

COOKING FOOD

While you can eat many of the meats raw, it is better to cook them as this will greatly increase the amount of health and saturation recovered. You can cook food using a furnace, campfire or smoker. Smokers cook twice as fast as a furnace but with half the experience, and campfires can cook four items at a time without the need for fuel.

STEWS

Stews are more nourishing than plain meat but also require more resources. Craft a bowl for your stew using three planks, then try out these two recipes:

Rabbit stew recipe

Mushroom stew recipe

Add a flower to your mushroom stew recipe grid to create a suspicious stew with a random status effect!

MOB	BREED WITH	FOOD
CHICKEN	WHEAT SEEDS / MELON SEEDS / BEETROOT SEEDS / PUMPKIN SEEDS	2 | 6 *Raw chicken can be poisonous and cause the Hunger effect.*
SHEEP	WHEAT	2 | 6
RABBIT	CARROT / GOLDEN CARROT / DANDELION	3 | 5
PIG	CARROTS / POTATOES / BEETROOTS	3 | 8
HOGLIN	CRIMSON FUNGUS	3 | 8
COW	WHEAT	3 | 8

29

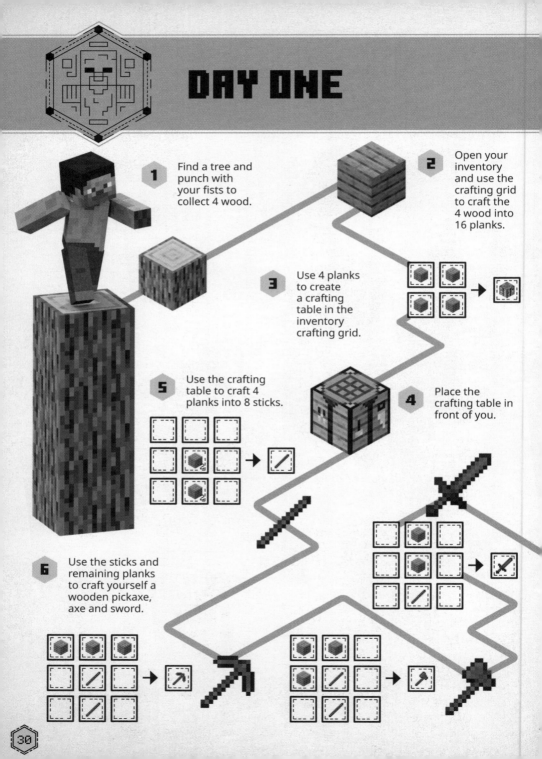

1 Find a tree and punch with your fists to collect 4 wood.

2 Open your inventory and use the crafting grid to craft the 4 wood into 16 planks.

3 Use 4 planks to create a crafting table in the inventory crafting grid.

4 Place the crafting table in front of you.

5 Use the crafting table to craft 4 planks into 8 sticks.

6 Use the sticks and remaining planks to craft yourself a wooden pickaxe, axe and sword.

Now that you know the basics, let's jump into the game. Your first day in the Overworld will be challenging, but if you move quickly and gather resources, you can set yourself up before night falls. This step-by-step guide will help you to embark on your first Minecraft journey.

13 When the sun goes down, use your bed to sleep until morning.

12 Place the bed inside your home and use it to save your respawn point.

11 Return to the crafting table and create a bed using wool and planks.

9 Create a landmark beside your home. A tall stack of blocks can easily be seen from afar to help you find your home when exploring.

8 Use your crafting table and 6 planks to craft a door for your home.

7 Use your axe to chop down more wood and create a simple home.

10 Search for some sheep and defeat them using your sword. Collect the raw mutton and wool they drop. You need 3 wool.

DAY TWO

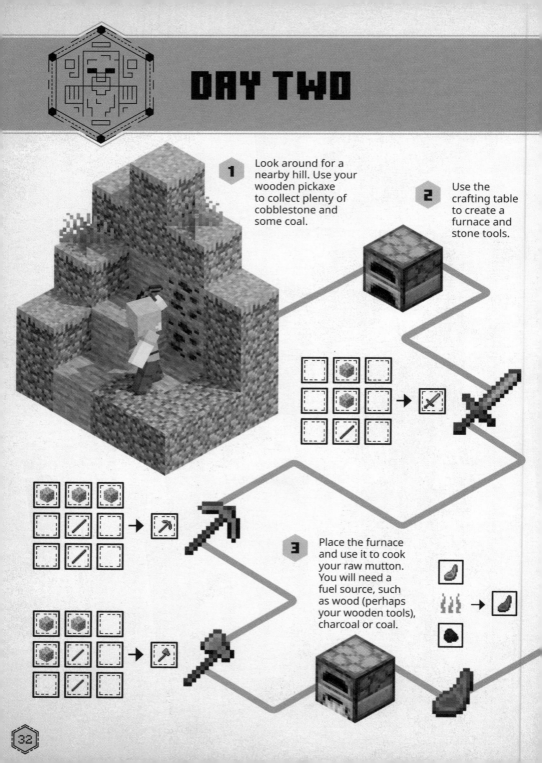

1 Look around for a nearby hill. Use your wooden pickaxe to collect plenty of cobblestone and some coal.

2 Use the crafting table to create a furnace and stone tools.

3 Place the furnace and use it to cook your raw mutton. You will need a fuel source, such as wood (perhaps your wooden tools), charcoal or coal.

Well done – you survived your first night! But that was just the first step. Continue to set up your base by searching for new materials and – just as important – food! There are plenty of resources to be found to satisfy your hunger bar and give you materials for your home.

8 Search for a cave and venture underground to find iron, using torches to light the way. Use the stone pickaxe to mine iron ore.

7 Craft yourself a torch with coal and a stick. If you can't find coal, charcoal can be made as a substitute by smelting logs in a furnace.

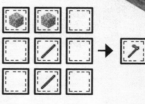

6 Search for a nearby water source, and use a hoe on grass blocks to create farmland around the water. Plant your seeds.

4 Eat the cooked meat to replenish the hunger bar.

5 Explore the area for useful resources. Collect any seeds and vegetables you can find to start your first farm.

9 Return to your home and place the raw iron and a fuel source in the furnace.

11 Return to the furnace and collect the smelted iron ingots.

10 Harvest any fully grown crops on your farm and plant new seeds.

12 Use iron ingots to craft tools such as a pickaxe, axe, sword, and shears.

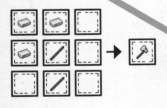

15 Continue your Minecraft adventure – what will you do next?

14 Sleep in the bed when it gets dark.

13 If you have any time left, use leftover collected wood to craft yourself additional items to aid your chances of survival, such as a bowl for stews, a boat for traveling on water, a chest to store your items in and fences to put up for your protection.

INTO THE GAME

Now that you've started your world, it's time to step deeper into it. There's a ton of exciting content to uncover in Minecraft and it's completely up to you to decide what you want to discover first. In this section we will take a closer look at what this blocky world has to offer, from biomes and generated structures to brewing and enchanting. Where will your adventure take you?

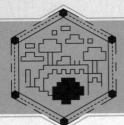
MERGING BIOMES

You can see the edges where biomes merge to form unique features in the landscape.

DESERT

This warm biome is formed mainly of sand with only cacti and dead bushes for vegetation, making survival here difficult. As expected, larger bodies of water are rare in this biome and you are more likely to come across a pond of lava than one of water.

JUNGLE

Though rare, jungles are abundant with lush vegetation and rich in wildlife. This biome is covered by a thick canopy of trees, including giant 2x2 jungle trees that can grow exceptionally tall, up to 31 blocks high. It is a very dense biome and difficult to build in.

The Overworld is the dimension where you first spawn in a new game. It's a place of blue skies and scudding clouds, under which lie a world full of rich biomes, diverse in their landscapes, vegetation and mobs, all waiting to be discovered. Let's take a look at some biomes you'll find on your journey.

FOREST

Forests are a popular choice for starting a new Survival world due to their abundance of oak and birch trees, as well as oodles of flowers and mobs to discover. It's also one of the most common biomes.

SAVANNA

This flat biome has a warm climate that doesn't see rain, meaning there's no worry of lightning – though it is not without its clouds. It is a great place to find resources, such as acacia trees for wood, horses for riding and llamas for pack animals.

PLAINS

The most popular biome for starting a Survival world, plains biomes have large open spaces for building and abundant wildlife for food. It is often easy to find nearby villages, too, as the open space allows you to see for a good distance in every direction.

TUNDRA

These cold, snowy biomes have fewer trees and mobs than elsewhere, making them a challenge for Survival mode. However, they do offer large, flat plains with plenty of room for building.

BADLANDS

The badlands biome, also known as mesa, is a rare warm biome consisting primarily of red sand with terracotta hills and mountains. Finding one will be tricky, but if you do, there's a chance you'll be rewarded as gold ore generates more commonly in this biome. However, it is similarly barren like deserts, with only cacti and dead bushes growing.

SWAMP

These flat, marsh-like biomes are full of shallow, murky waters and wildlife, including frogs. Slimes spawn here most often, especially during a full moon.

MOUNTAINS

Mountains are split into two subcategories: extreme hills and mountain peaks. They are made up of sky-high elevations and sheer drops. Besides the windswept hills biome, emerald ore is found only in the tall peaks of mountains biomes.

MUSHROOM FIELDS

Easily the rarest and most bizarre-looking biome in the Overworld, mushroom fields usually generate as islands. Instead of grass and trees, this biome is covered with mycelium and enormous mushrooms. It is also home to mooshrooms – a strange, mushroom-covered cow variant.

TAIGA

The taiga biome is very similar to the forest biome, but it is colder, has a bluish hue and darker waters, and is filled with ferns and spruce trees. Here, you'll find small quantities of sweet berry bushes, pumpkins and foxes.

BEACHES

Wherever an ocean meets a biome, one of three beaches will generate depending on the temperature and height of the biome it skirts: beach, stony shore and snowy beach. Buried treasure often generates under the sand, and large copper ore veins are common here.

RIVERS

Thin, long and winding, river biomes generate between biomes and either feed from the ocean or form in loops. They have an abundance of water, sand, gravel and clay, making them a resourceful place to start your Survival journey.

OCEANS

Just like in the real world, oceans cover the largest area in the Overworld – nearly a third! This biome stretches all the way down to the ocean floor, making it immense. Survival is possible but challenging, with fish and kelp forests for food and underwater ravines to mine for blocks.

RARE VARIANT

You might stumble across an ice spikes biome. This is a rare variant of the snowy plains, which features many shards of ice jutting out from its landscape. No trees or buildings will ever generate here, making it one of the least forgiving places to roam in the Overworld.

SNOWY PLAINS

A snow-covered grassland biome, snowy plains are a challenging place to survive, with powder snow to freeze unwary travelers and slippery blue ice to make movement difficult. Very few mobs live here, and farming is challenging as water sources will freeze to ice, making farmland irrigation incredibly difficult.

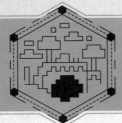

GENERATED STRUCTURES: OVERWORLD

VILLAGE

Communities of villagers live across the Overworld. Villages are found in most biomes and are filled with useful job sites. You can trade your resources with the villagers for useful blocks, items and tools.

DESERT PYRAMID

These large sandstone buildings can be found in desert biomes. If you search around, you'll find a secret room containing four chests. Watch your step – they're protected by a TNT trap!

JUNGLE TEMPLE

Overgrown with jungle leaves and vines, these cobblestone structures are found hidden in jungle biomes. They contain a redstone puzzle that, if solved, will reveal two chests full of loot.

As you venture through the biomes, you're going to stumble across many generated structures – buildings, which are usually occupied. You'll spot different structures on land, below ground and even underwater. Finding these can reward you with loot – but watch out! Some are rife with danger.

WOODLAND MANSION

A massive, three-story, dark oak building filled with many rooms and loot chests. Find one using an explorer map. Be warned, though, this rare structure is defended by vindicators and evokers.

PILLAGER OUTPOST

Keep an eye out for outposts – though heavily guarded by crossbow-wielding pillagers, they can generate with caged iron golems and allays, as well as other loot – a worthy and valuable reward.

STRONGHOLD

Buried deep underground, strongholds are maze-like structures made of stone bricks. There are many rooms to explore, and somewhere inside the stronghold will be an unactivated End portal that you can repair to reach the End.

OCEAN MONUMENT

This massive prismarine structure can be found deep underwater. They're home to guardians and elder guardians that will chase any explorer away. However, the structure contains a room with eight blocks of gold in it and potentially some sponges, which are great for mopping up water.

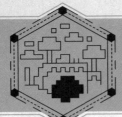

MOB ENCOUNTERS: OVERWORLD

MOB INTERACTIONS

No matter how you play Survival mode, interacting with mobs will be hugely beneficial to your progress. Whether they're passive, neutral or hostile, there are rewards to be earned for getting to know your fellow world inhabitants.

SPAWNING

Mobs will spawn naturally throughout the Overworld depending on the light level. In general, most passive (friendly) and neutral mobs will spawn in bright areas, while hostile (dangerous) mobs will spawn in dark areas.

EXPERIENCE & DROPS

Defeated mobs can drop loot such as XP orbs and items that you can use for crafting recipes and enchanting items. Some dropped loot cannot be found elsewhere. XP is used when enchanting (see page 66).

TAMING

Some mobs, such as cats, horses and llamas, can be tamed into loyal companions by feeding them their favorite food, while others, such as axolotls and foxes, can be persuaded to trust you. Once tamed, they will follow you, and wolves will even aid you in battle.

BREEDING

Some mobs of the world can be bred by giving them certain foods. Feeding two mobs of the same species will cause them to produce offspring.

It won't be long before you encounter one of the many mobs that roam the Overworld. Some of these mobs can become helpful companions, while others will be intent on causing your demise. No matter their temperament, they will all prove useful on your adventure.

MOB KEY

In the coming pages, you'll meet many of the mobs you'll encounter in Minecraft. Each mob has different health and damage stats, as well as different items that they drop if defeated and foods that can be used to tame and breed them. Look out for these icons beside each mob profile on the following pages to discover their stats in Bedrock Edition.

20

The heart stat signifies the maximum hit points a mob can take before they are defeated.

6

The sword is the maximum damage a mob can dish out at melee range on Normal difficulty. This can increase on Hard.

11

The bow is the maximum damage a mob can do long-range on Normal. This can also increase on Hard.

2

Some mobs have armor to protect them. The armor stat is how much protection the mob has from their gear.

arrow		experience orb		ominous banner		scute
beetroot		feather		phantom membrane		seagrass
blaze rod		flowers		poppy		shulker shell
bone		glass bottle		potato		head
bone meal		glow berries		pufferfish		spider eye
bowl		glowstone dust		rabbit's foot		sticks
bread		goat horn		rabbit hide		string
carrot		golden axe		raw beef		sugar
coal		golden carrot		raw chicken		sweet berries
copper ingot		golden sword		raw cod		totem of undying
crossbow		gunpowder		raw porkchop		trident
dandelion		iron ingot		raw rabbit		tropical fish
egg		leather		raw salmon		wheat
emerald		magma cream		redstone dust		Wither skeleton skull
enchanted book		music disk		rotten flesh		
Ender pearl		nautilus shell		saddle		

PASSIVE MOBS

These mobs are harmless and will not attack players, even when provoked. Most passive mobs are tameable or breedable, making them highly useful mobs to have around as companions and farm animals.

VILLAGER

Helpful villagefolk that exchange goods for emeralds.	♥ 20	👕 2

Breed
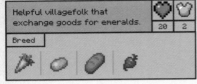

SHEEP

This mob is the only natural source of wool, which is great for beds, carpets and decorating. Found in most grassy biomes.	♥ 8

Breed	Drops

SALMON

Found in oceans and rivers, this mob is a great source of food.	♥ 6

Drops

SEA TURTLE

An aquatic mob that will always return to its home beach to lay eggs and drops a scute when it grows up.	♥ 30

Breed	Drops

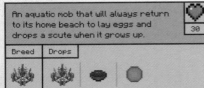

CHICKEN

Flightless birds that spawn in grassy areas and will follow you around if you hold out seeds.

♥ 4

Breed

Drops

PIG

Common within grassy biomes, pigs can be saddled and ridden.

♥ 10

Breed

Drops

RABBIT

Rabbits hop around aimlessly and love carrots so much, they will jump off a cliff just to reach one.

♥ 3

Breed

Drops

COW

This large mob can be milked with a bucket and is found in almost all grassy biomes.

♥ 10

Breed | **Drops**

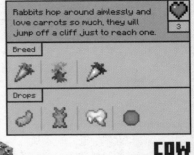

CAT

Not a cat person? Neither are creepers, which will avoid them. Cats will approach you if you are holding a raw fish.

♥ 10

Breed/Tame | **Drops**

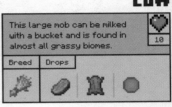

FOX

A nocturnal mob that pounces on its prey and can carry a single item in its mouth.

♥ 20

Breed/Tame | **Drops**

HORSE

Persistence is needed to tame this friendly mob – you need to mount it repeatedly until it no longer bucks you off. Only then can you saddle and ride it.

♥ 30

Breed | **Drops**

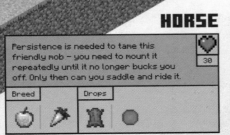
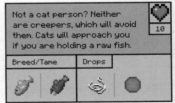
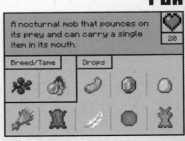

NEUTRAL MOBS

Neutral mobs are normally harmless toward players but will become hostile if provoked. Some only become aggressive when attacked, while others can be provoked in different ways.

POLAR BEAR

As cute as they are, steer clear of cubs, as this mob attacks those who go near its young.	30	5

Drops

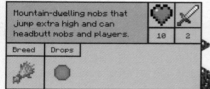

GOAT

Mountain-dwelling mobs that jump extra high and can headbutt mobs and players.	10	2

Breed | Drops

SPIDER

Though terrifyingly huge for a spider, this mob only becomes hostile in low light.	16	2

Drops

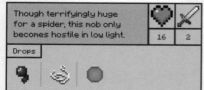

DOLPHIN

Feed this mob raw fish and it will lead you to the nearest treasure, but cross it and you'll have an entire pod to answer to.	10	3

Drops

WOLF

This mob is easily tamed and will follow you and aid you in battle. They are particularly hostile toward skeletons.

❤️	⚔️
20	4

Breed/Tame	Drops
🦴	⚫

IRON GOLEM

These warriors defend players and villagers from hostile threats and can spawn poppies to gift to villagers.

❤️	⚔️
100	21.5

Drops	
▱	⚘

BEE

These cute mobs pollinate plants and are a source of honey – careful, though, as they don't give it up willingly!

❤️	⚔️
10	2

Breed	Drops
🌻	⚫

HOSTILE MOBS

Of course, not all mobs are friendly; some will attack players on sight. Biomes and structures can contain different threats across the Overworld, so it's wise to learn what you're up against! If you're lucky, an armored mob will also drop its equipment when defeated.

CREEPER

This sneaky mob creeps up on players and explodes to deal massive damage.

♥	⚔
20	85

Drops

SKELETON

An undead, bow-wielding mob that shoots arrows at players.

♥	⚔	⛏
20	2	4

Drops

HUSK

A desiccated variant of the zombie, which shambles across desert sands and can survive in sunlight.

♥	⚔	🦺
20	3	2

Drops

DROWNED

This zombie variant spawns underwater, swimming up at night to haunt shores. It sometimes carries a trident.

♥	⚔	⛏	🦺
20	11	9	2

Drops

PHANTOM

Be sure to rest up as this winged mob spawns after you go three nights without sleep.

❤️	⚔️
20	6

Drops
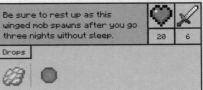

WITCH

This mob may look like a friendly villager, but don't be fooled – it throws nasty potions at you.

❤️	⚔️
26	6

Drops
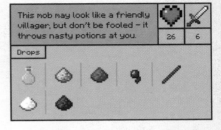

PILLAGER

Crossbow-wielding illagers that raid villages and guard outposts containing loot.

❤️	⚔️	⛏️
24	3	4

Drops

RAVAGER

Spawning during illager raids, this beast rams enemies with its hefty head and can only be ridden by illagers.

❤️	⚔️
100	12

Drops
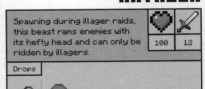

EVOKER

A spell-casting illager that is found in woodland mansions and raids, and attacks with fangs or vexes.

❤️	⚔️	🛡️
24	6	2

Drops
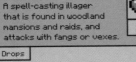

VINDICATOR

This iron axe-wielding illager is found in woodland mansions and participates in raids.

❤️	⚔️
24	13

Drops

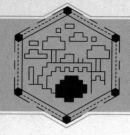

DEFEND YOURSELF!

ARMOR

Your first defense against hostile mobs is your equipment. Each piece of armor will cumulatively reduce the damage that mobs and other threats can do to you.

TOP TIP

Did you know that an unarmored player can be killed instantly by an exploding creeper?

These can be swapped if you want your character to be left-handed.

MAIN HAND

OFF-HAND

CHESTPLATE

LEGGINGS

ARMOR POINTS

Each piece of armor you wear gives you armor points, which reduce the damage you receive. If you're wearing a full set of the same armor, you'll get bonus armor points, too. Both diamond and netherite armor can provide the full 20 armor points, but netherite gives better protection against strong attacks.

BOOTS

With so many threats awaiting you on your adventures, it's vital that you're prepared for any confrontation. A good sword and shield will help keep you alive, but there's more that you can do to defend yourself and your home. Good preparation will greatly increase your chances of survival.

STRUCTURAL DEFENSE

Keeping yourself safe is a challenge, but keeping your home safe is even more difficult. You wouldn't want to return home to find a creeper in your bedroom! Luckily, there are some countermeasures you can take to keep your home mob-free.

LIGHTING

Hostile mobs will only spawn in dark areas. By placing torches or other light sources at regular intervals around your home, you can eliminate dark spaces and prevent hostile mobs from spawning.

WALLS & FENCES

One sure way to keep mobs away is to build two-block-tall walls. Alternatively, if a wall isn't the look you're after, fences around your base will keep most mobs at bay, besides those with ranged attacks.

DOORSTEPS

Watch out for zombies banging on your door – in Hard mode, enough hits and it will break! You can stop them in their tracks with a simple trick: a doorstep. Place your door above ground level and zombies' attacks will not be able to damage it.

TOP TIP

Looking for more defenses? Check out enchanting and brewing on pages 66–69.

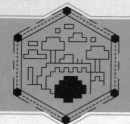

BATTLING MOBS

SWORD & SHIELD

A sword attack will make quick work of dispatching mobs. Keep an eye on the attack cooldown – a full charge will deliver a devastating blow. When being attacked, raise your shield to block the incoming damage.

TOOLS

If you are caught unprepared, some tools, such as axes, pickaxes and shovels, can also be wielded to great effect.

TRIDENT

A trident can be wielded both in melee and range, making it a very valuable weapon indeed! It cannot be crafted – a trident must be obtained by defeating drowned mobs who have one.

BOW & CROSSBOW

Some mobs are better off eliminated from a safe distance. For example, if you let a creeper get too close, it'll explode and could even take you down with it. Be careful you don't run out of arrows!

Should you find yourself face-to-face with a hostile mob, you will have two options: fight or flight. A steady retreat is a good defense, but when cornered, you may have to rely on your sword to make it out alive. If you find yourself caught without a chance of escape, remember your training!

TERRAIN TACTICS

Use the terrain to your advantage. Mobs are not player-controlled and can easily be fooled with a few simple tricks:

Flying mobs and tall mobs cannot reach you if you're sheltered under a roof. Building a roof above your head will prevent Endermen and phantoms from reaching you – but you will also be pinned down for other mobs to attack.

In desperate moments, you can also build a quick shelter and battle mobs from safety. A 3x3 chamber like this will keep you safe on all sides and even allow you to attack the mobs. Most mobs cannot reach you – apart from small mobs such as baby zombies. Keep an eye out for these little menaces and be sure to eliminate them first.

Many mobs cannot climb, so getting to high ground can keep you safe. In a pinch, you can stack two blocks to raise yourself into the air and then use your sword to eliminate the mobs below. You can hit them, but they can't hit you.

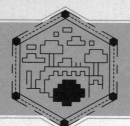

FIND YOUR WAY

1 USE THE SUN!

Just like in the real world, you can rely on the sun's position to navigate the Overworld. With the understanding that the sun and moon rise in the east and set in the west, that clouds always travel westward and that the stars also turn westward, you can figure out your direction without a compass.

2 SAVE YOUR COORDINATES

You can display the block position of your character in the top-left corner of the screen by selecting Show Coordinates in the World Options menu. The X indicates longitude, the Y indicates latitude and the Z indicates elevation. Simply write down the coordinates of your home, and if you ever get lost, you can then navigate back to those coordinates.

3 LANDMARKS

Getting a feel for the layout of your local area will help you keep track of where you are and where you need to go. Look around for distinctive landmarks, such as rivers, mountains and biomes. You can also create your own landmarks, such as block towers that can be seen from a great distance, so that you'll always be able to find your way back there.

Exploring Minecraft is a breathtaking experience. As you march through jungles, swamps and mountains in search of resources, the beauty can be distracting — so much so that it's easy to lose track of where you are. Luckily, there are a few tricks you can use to navigate.

4 MAPS

You should always aim to carry a locator map that was crafted with a compass. It records the local area as you explore, creating a visual guide to help you navigate, as well as showing you where you are on it. It even updates if the terrain changes, meaning new structures will appear on it, too – you'll never struggle to find your way back to your base again!

5 TORCH TRAIL

Venturing underground poses fresh exploration challenges, such as never-ending tunnels that will disorient even the most experienced players. To help keep track of where you've been and which way it is to the exit, place torches on the right-hand wall as you descend. To retrace your steps, simply follow the torches back to the surface.

6 SET A RESPAWN POINT

Lastly, the easiest and surest way to ensure you can always return home is to save your respawn point by using a bed. If you ever lose your home, respawning will return you to your bed. This should only be used as a last resort, as you will respawn without any of your items or inventory. That's a steep price to pay!

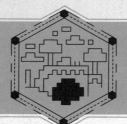

GO THE DISTANCE

TOP TIP

You can increase your movement speed with potions and enchantments (see pages 66–69).

WALKING, SPRINTING & SWIMMING

You can explore the old-fashioned way – on two feet! Walking and swimming are the simplest ways to get around. If you're in a rush, you can sprint to speed up your journey, but stock up on food as it's hungry work!

RIDING

Riding is a great way to cross large distances quickly. First you'll have to find a horse, mule, donkey, strider or pig, and a saddle. Saddles cannot be crafted but can be found by looting generated structures or trading for them from leatherworker villagers. Not all mobs are ridden in the same way, but they will generally need taming first (see page 46). Some mobs, such as donkeys, mules and llamas, can even equip chests for extra storage.

MINECARTS

If you take the same route often, you could connect the two destinations with a railway using rails and a minecart. Your railway will allow you to travel back and forth with ease and speed, and can also be used as a supply line using minecarts with chests.

The world is huge, and you will soon find yourself crossing vast distances in search of resources, biomes and generated structures. Depending on how far you need to travel, you'll want to consider the best way to reach your destination. Thankfully, there are plenty of ways to get around.

NETHER PORTAL HUB

The quickest and most efficient way to travel great distances is by Nether portal. However, a word of caution: The Nether is a dangerous place (see pages 72-79). You will also need to craft a diamond pickaxe in order to mine the obsidian you need to build the portal frames.

A Nether portal hub works in a simple way: For every block traveled in the Nether, you will travel eight blocks in the Overworld. For example, if you travel 100 blocks in the Nether to a second portal, you will have traveled 800 blocks in the same direction across the Overworld.

Because the Nether is filled with fiery lakes and dangerous mobs, many players like to climb to the highest level of the Nether to build their portal hub.

TOP TIP

Pack a flint and steel when entering a portal. If your portal gets damaged, you will need to reignite it, or you will get stuck in the Nether dimension.

GET TO KNOW THE VILLAGERS

WHERE TO FIND THEM

Villagers are found in villages in plains, tundra, savanna, desert and taiga biomes, and their appearance will differ depending on where they come from. You may even see zombified villagers roaming the Overworld. They can be cured with a golden apple.

TRADING

Every employed villager will be willing to trade with you. The items they offer will depend on their profession – see next page. You can trade blocks and items for emeralds, or emeralds for blocks and items.

SKILLED MERCHANTS

Trading with villagers will give them experience, increasing their rank and unlocking better trades. Their prices change with demand, and they can sell out of items until they've had a chance to craft more. They all begin as novices and can become apprentices, journeymen and finally experts.

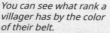

| NOVICE | APPRENTICE | JOURNEYMAN | EXPERT |

You can see what rank a villager has by the color of their belt.

Villagers are more than just friendly faces – they have a treasure trove of valuable items to trade and are enormously helpful. They offer everything from emeralds to enchanted books and explorer maps, so getting to know your village neighbors can be hugely rewarding.

JOBS

Other than the energetic baby villagers and nitwits, villagers are busy workers that will seek out employment. If you see an unemployed villager wearing their plain robes, place a job block to give them a profession.

Nitwits are villagers that cannot gain a profession.

	ARMORER Trades powerful armor and shields.			**LEATHERWORKER** Buys leather and makes leather armor and saddles from it.
	BUTCHER Buys raw foods and sells cooked ones.			**LIBRARIAN** Buys books and sells enchanted books.
	CARTOGRAPHER Sells explorer maps and banners.			**STONE MASON** Buys stone and clay and sells various decorated blocks.
	CLERIC Buys rotten flesh and sells items such as lapis lazuli and Ender pearls.			**SHEPHERD** Buys wool and sells beds and banners.
	FARMER Buys and sells food, including cake and golden carrots.			**TOOLSMITH** Sells enchanted tools.
	FISHERMAN Buys raw fish and sells cooked fish and enchanted fishing rods.			**WEAPONSMITH** Sells enchanted swords and axes.
	FLETCHER Sells enchanted bows and crossbows.			

NEW JOB

You can change the job of any villager that you haven't yet traded with. Simply destroy their job block and place down a new one. This will change their profession. If the same job block is placed, it will refresh their trades.

GOSSIP & REPUTATION

Just like any community living together, villagers love to gossip. They will talk about all your good and bad deeds and even tell other villagers about them when they meet. Your reputation is important, as it will affect the prices offered when trading.

POSITIVE actions, such as curing and trading, will increase your reputation.

NEGATIVE actions such as attacking and killing, will decrease your reputation.

IRON DEFENDER

Villagers are very helpful but also very vulnerable. Luckily, they can call upon the help of iron golems to keep them safe from hostile mobs. If a village has at least 10 villagers and 20 beds, an iron golem will be spawned to protect the people.

POPULARITY

Always respect your neighbors. Mistreat villagers and it won't just be your reputation that decreases but also your popularity in the village as a whole. If your popularity drops too low, then the naturally spawned iron golems protecting the village will turn on you and attack.

EXPANDING YOUR VILLAGE

Trading with villagers will reward you with many useful items that you need to stay alive. Though villages in the Overworld will spawn with villagers in them, you will need the support of a full village with every job in it to raise your chances of survival. You can increase the population of villages by encouraging the villagers to have children.

VILLAGE TRANSFORMATION

In order to increase the population of a village, start by creating the perfect living conditions for the villagers, which will make them more willing to procreate. Here is a simple way to transform a village home into a setting that may persuade two villagers to have children.

BEDS

Villagers need beds for their new offspring or they won't breed. Place additional beds for every new villager you wish to welcome to the village.

DOORS

Don't forget a door, so that your villagers can get outside to tend to their crops – you don't want them to starve!

FOOD

A well-fed villager is a happy villager. Create some farmland with a water source, and plant some carrots, potatoes or beetroots. Place a composter, and a villager will soon start farming to provide the household with all the food they need. Just make sure one villager is a farmer!

TOP TIP

Villagers cannot open fence gates. Place a pressure plate to keep the gate closed and your villagers safe from hostile mobs.

ENCHANT YOUR TOOLS

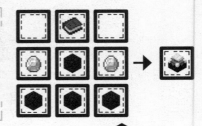

HOW DO I ENCHANT?

To be able to enchant, you will need an enchanting table. You can craft these using a book, 2 diamonds and 4 obsidian blocks. You will then need a tool or piece of equipment to enchant, 1–3 pieces of lapis lazuli and some experience levels to begin enchanting with your new table.

USING AN ENCHANTING TABLE

Enchanted tables offer randomized enchantments that depend on the item being enchanted and the number of bookcases nearby. When you interact with a table, the following user interface will appear:

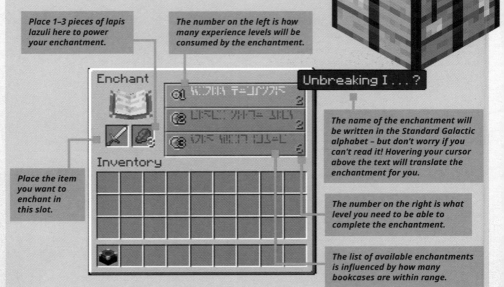

Place 1–3 pieces of lapis lazuli here to power your enchantment.

The number on the left is how many experience levels will be consumed by the enchantment.

Place the item you want to enchant in this slot.

Unbreaking I . . . ?

The name of the enchantment will be written in the Standard Galactic alphabet – but don't worry if you can't read it! Hovering your cursor above the text will translate the enchantment for you.

The number on the right is what level you need to be able to complete the enchantment.

The list of available enchantments is influenced by how many bookcases are within range.

The quickest way to improve your gear is to find a stronger material; however, the best way to improve gear is by enchanting it. There are lots of different enchantments, ranging from more durable tools to more powerful swords. Enchanting is rewarding but expensive!

BROADENING YOUR KNOWLEDGE

We all know that the more you read, the more knowledgeable you are. The same works for enchanting tables! If you place bookshelves around your table – up to 15 – you will unlock more powerful enchantments, which will unlock everything up to level 30 enchantments.

ENCHANTED BOOKS

You can find most enchantments with an enchanting table; however, some enchantments such as Mending and Frost Walker, can only be traded as enchanted books from villagers. You can add these to items using an anvil.

ENCHANTMENTS

There are 37 unique enchantments you can use on your equipment, and you can even have multiple enchantments on one piece of gear. Some enchantments can be applied to multiple items while others are limited to specific ones. Here are some of the most useful Survival mode enchantments to look out for:

EFFICIENCY
Increases how fast you can mine.

UNBREAKING
Increases the durability of items.

SMITE
Increases damage against undead mobs.

FEATHER FALLING
Reduces fall damage.

INFINITY
Prevents arrows from being consumed.

IT'S POTION TIME

HOW DO I BREW?

Most potions are the result of multiple brewing steps, transforming your potion from one state to another and then to the one you want. First, you need a brewing stand. These can be found in igloos and villages, and can be crafted using a blaze rod and cobblestone. Blaze rods can be looted from blazes (see page 78), which you will also need for blaze powder to fuel your brewing stand. You will then need glass bottles and a water source such as a cauldron for filling them with water.

BREWING PROCESS

1 Fill your glass bottles with water from a cauldron and place them into the three brewing slots. Put blaze powder into the fuel slot – the number shows how many you have remaining.

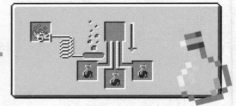

2 Create a base potion. Awkward potions are the base of the majority of potions and don't have an effect on their own. You can make these by placing a Nether wart in the ingredient slot.

3 Now pick an ingredient to add an effect to your base potions and place it in the ingredient slot. Sugar added to Awkward potions will create potions of Swiftness.

4 Move the brewed potions from the brewing stand and put them into your inventory. Try other ingredients to see what potions you can create.

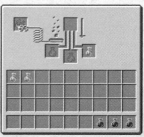

By the time you've spent a few weeks in Minecraft, you will undoubtedly have faced many dangerous threats and wished you were better prepared. With brewing, you can craft many potions that will aid you on your Survival journey, from a Potion of Fire Resistance to a Potion of Healing.

HERE ARE JUST SOME OF THE POTIONS YOU CAN CREATE TO AID YOUR CHANCES OF SURVIVAL:

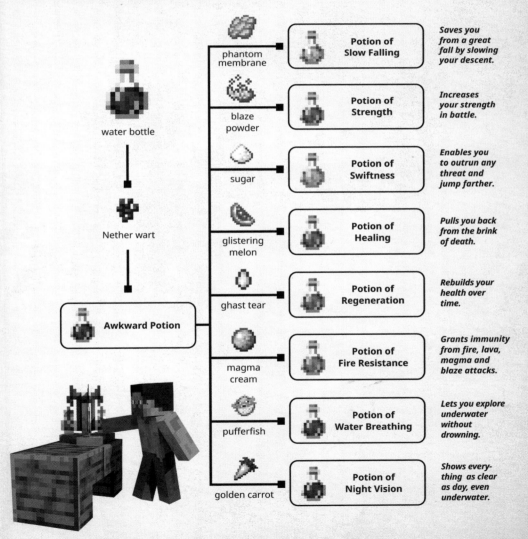

water bottle

Nether wart

Awkward Potion

phantom membrane

Potion of Slow Falling
Saves you from a great fall by slowing your descent.

blaze powder

Potion of Strength
Increases your strength in battle.

sugar

Potion of Swiftness
Enables you to outrun any threat and jump farther.

glistering melon

Potion of Healing
Pulls you back from the brink of death.

ghast tear

Potion of Regeneration
Rebuilds your health over time.

magma cream

Potion of Fire Resistance
Grants immunity from fire, lava, magma and blaze attacks.

pufferfish

Potion of Water Breathing
Lets you explore underwater without drowning.

golden carrot

Potion of Night Vision
Shows everything as clear as day, even underwater.

NEW DIMENSIONS

As you continue to develop your home in the Overworld,
you'll become stronger and readier to face bigger
challenges. It's time to discover two alternative
dimensions: the Nether and the End. These dimensions
are dangerous and strange, but also wondrous and
unlike anything you'll have experienced in the
Overworld – not to mention they're full of loot you won't
find elsewhere! Reaching and exploring these dimensions
will put your survival skills to the test as you encounter
the many perils of the Nether and face down the
infamous Ender Dragon in the End dimension.

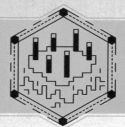

THE NETHER

REACHING THE NETHER

To reach the Nether, you will need to create a Nether portal. You can do this by repairing a ruined portal or creating a new one using obsidian blocks to build a rectangular shape and igniting it with a flint and steel.

Crying obsidian will stop your portal from working, so it needs replacing.

You can mine obsidian using a diamond pickaxe or create it by flowing lava into a water source block.

You need to ignite it with a flint and steel.

Portal build diagram

RESPAWN POINT

Once in the Nether, you may be tempted to sleep in a bed and save your respawn point – DO NOT TRY THIS! It's impossible to sleep in this nightmare dimension, and attempts to do so will result in your bed exploding. To save your respawn point, you'll need a respawn anchor made of crying obsidian and glowstone.

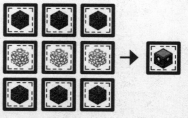

Respawn anchor recipe

As you are exploring the Overworld, you might stumble across a ruined portal. Repairing it will create a gateway to the Nether dimension, a land full of fire, lava and fungus – or you can make one from scratch. Proceed with caution, though – this is a perilous dimension.

LOCAL INHABITANTS

The Nether's mobs are just as unwelcoming as its landscapes, with many hostile mobs such as ghasts that will shoot explosive fireballs at you and Wither skeletons that will aim to inflict you with the Wither effect. However, there are also some mobs that with some effort can become your allies, such as piglins that will barter with you for gold ingots.

ancient debris

glowstone

netherrack

quartz

ANCIENT DEBRIS

Exploring the Nether will reward you with new blocks to build with. If you're lucky, you'll even find ancient debris. Ancient debris can be smelted into netherite scraps that, when combined with gold ingots, will produce netherite ingots. You can use these to upgrade to the best armor and weapons.

NEW MOUNTS

You might wish to bring your horse to the Nether, but the tough terrain and huge lava lakes are not suited to their movement. Thankfully, you can find striders in the Nether. These cute mobs will do anything for some mushrooms, even walk across lava! Put a saddle on a strider and use a warped fungus on a stick to guide it around.

73

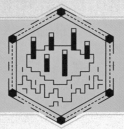

BIOMES:
THE NETHER

SOUL SAND VALLEY

The Nether equivalent of a desert, this biome is covered with soul sand that slows players down. If that wasn't enough, soul fire – a powerful blue flame – also ravages the land. Keep an eye out for the fossil remains of ancient creatures.

CRIMSON FOREST

This biome is named after the crimson fungus that grows abundantly on its surface. Unusual for the mostly barren Nether, this biome has its own ecosystem and is full of piglins and hoglins.

NETHER WASTES

This is the most common biome in the Nether. It is covered with netherrack and ore deposits, but it is also dominated by dangerous zombified piglins.

PORTAL

Once you're done facing dangers and collecting loot, you can return to the Overworld through a portal, and find out just how far you've traveled (see page 61).

The Nether is a dangerous place with a rugged terrain that makes exploration a challenge. However, among the biomes there is beauty and wonder to be discovered, as well as many useful items such as blaze rods, which are key to accessing the End dimension and for brewing potions.

BASALT DELTA

Possibly the most dangerous of biomes in the Nether, basalt deltas consist of steep, spiky basalt formations interspersed with pools of lava. Proceed with caution!

WARPED FOREST

As far as the Nether goes, this biome is relatively safe. Its rich flora may even seem like a good place to settle down; however, the many grieving Endermen that roam around will be hazardous to both your buildings and your peace.

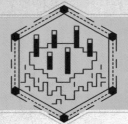

LAVA LAKES

Huge lava lakes are present in some Nether biomes. You do not want to fall into these! It only takes moments for your health bar to drain and all your items to be destroyed by the heat. If you need to cross lava, build a bridge or ride a strider.

HIDDEN LAVA SPOUTS

Be careful where you go mining! There could be lava spouts hidden behind the netherrack walls. If you see lava coming toward you, quickly step back or stop it by placing a block. Unlike in the Overworld, you won't have water to douse the flames.

SOUL SAND

Soul sand can be found in the soul sand valley biome. It will slow you down when you walk across it, making you an easy target for mobs. If you have an enchanting table, you can enchant your boots with Soul Speed to enable you to run across it.

BASALT COLUMNS

These vertical columns are found in basalt delta biomes and are surrounded by lava. One misstep will have you swimming in the hot stuff. You can loot magma cream by defeating magma cubes, and use it to create potions of Fire Resistance.

The various biomes of the Nether are very different from those of the Overworld, so you'll need new strategies for exploring. Be sure to avoid charging around and jumping blindly over blocks – doing this will likely have you bumping into mobs, falling into lava pits or getting hopelessly lost.

TOP TIPS FOR EXPLORING THE NETHER

The rugged terrain makes exploration challenging. Before venturing out, prepare your inventory with some useful items and blocks.

FIRE RESISTANCE

You cannot have water in the Nether – it'll evaporate immediately. This makes fire all the more deadly! Prepare yourself with a handful of potions of Fire Resistance in case of emergency. They will save your life if you fall in lava.

SCAFFOLDING & BUILDING BLOCKS

The precipitous drops and wide canyons make traveling from biome to biome extremely difficult. Always set out with a few stacks of blocks to build bridges. Scaffolding is also useful for climbing mountainous facades.

GOLD EQUIPMENT

Piglins love gold. They love it so much, they even love players who wear gold. Keep yourself safe from them by wearing a piece of golden equipment. They'll leave you alone, as long as you don't touch their gold or chests.

MARKERS

It's easy to get lost in the Nether, more so than in the Overworld because you cannot create maps. Place a trail of markers whenever you go out exploring, so you can make your way back home.

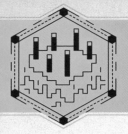

MOB ENCOUNTERS: THE NETHER

MAGMA CUBE

This hostile mob comes in 3 sizes. When defeated, it splits into 2-4 smaller magma cubes.

♥	⚔	🛡
1-16	3-6	3-12

Drops

BLAZE

Defeating this mob will get you useful blaze rods, but watch out for its fireball attack.

♥	⚔	⚔
20	5	6

Drops

WITHER SKELETON

This tall skeleton variant wields a stone sword and can inflict the Wither effect.

♥	⚔
20	8

Drops

GHAST

You'll likely hear this ghostly mob's cries before you see it. Avoid its exploding fireballs.

♥	⚔
10	12

Drops

Mobs in the Nether spawn far more frequently than those in the Overworld and are entirely unavoidable. Running away isn't always an option when you're surrounded by lava lakes, so it's advised that you go into battle with some knowledge of your enemy! See page 47 for the mob icon key.

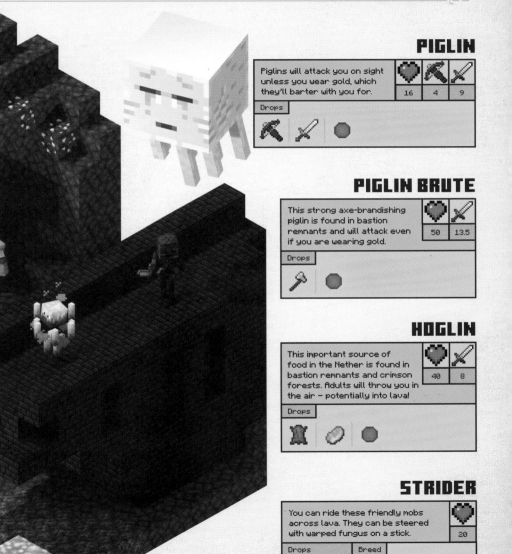

PIGLIN

Piglins will attack you on sight unless you wear gold, which they'll barter with you for.

❤	⛏	⚔
16	4	9

Drops

PIGLIN BRUTE

This strong axe-brandishing piglin is found in bastion remnants and will attack even if you are wearing gold.

❤	⚔
50	13.5

Drops

HOGLIN

This important source of food in the Nether is found in bastion remnants and crimson forests. Adults will throw you in the air – potentially into lava!

❤	⚔
40	8

Drops

STRIDER

You can ride these friendly mobs across lava. They can be steered with warped fungus on a stick.

❤
20

Drops Breed

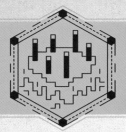

THE END

REACHING THE END

To reach the End, you must first find a stronghold in the Overworld and repair the End portal found inside. You can find strongholds by throwing Ender pearls and following which direction they go – they will point you directly to the closest stronghold. When they no longer go in any direction, dig down until you reach a mossy cobblestone structure beneath.

END PORTAL

Once inside the stronghold, search for a room with an End portal in it. The portal needs 12 eyes of Ender to become operational, which you can craft using Ender pearls and blaze powder. Once repaired, a star field against a black void will appear – jump in to travel to the End dimension.

Now that you've visited the Nether, are you ready to face one of the game's biggest challenges? Before embarking on this dangerous journey, make sure that you are prepared, for once you step into the portal, there is no going home until you have defeated the Ender Dragon – or it defeats you!

BATTLING THE ENDER DRAGON

Your first challenge upon entering the End is battling the Ender Dragon. Once you are victorious, End gateways appear, which allow you to explore the End, and an exit portal back to the Overworld is activated. Here are some tips for defeating the Ender Dragon:

END CRYSTALS

Your first step should be to destroy the End crystals perched atop the obsidian pillars. These will heal the Ender Dragon until shattered. Shoot them with a bow and arrow. Smashing them with a tool will also work but may prove fatal, as they explode on impact.

AVOID DRAGON BREATH

Avoid stepping near the pink flames of dragon breath at all costs! These pink flames will rapidly deplete your health bar.

ENDERMEN

Be sure to watch out for Endermen, too, as they are easily angered during the fight and can teleport to you.

AIM AT THE HEAD

When attacking, try to hit the Ender Dragon's head to deal full damage. Any hits to the body will only do minimal damage.

WATER BUCKET

Carry a bucket of water to save yourself from fall damage. The Ender Dragon will occasionally launch you high into the air, so using a water bucket as you land will save you from potentially fatal fall damage.

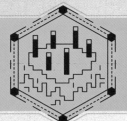

BIOMES:
THE END

THE CENTRAL ISLAND

Generated at the center of the End dimension, this is where you battle the Ender Dragon, and it contains the only exit portal out of the End and back to the Overworld.

END GATEWAYS

These portals appear after defeating the Ender Dragon and allow you to reach the outer islands of the End. You can travel through the portals by throwing an Ender pearl directly into one – but make sure to take an extra one with you because you'll need a pearl for the return journey. If you want to visit another End location, you can resummon the Ender Dragon and defeat it for another portal – up to 20. Imagine all the loot you'd find in 20 End locations!

Congratulations! The Ender Dragon has been defeated and the end credits have rolled. But your adventure does not end here! You have now unlocked an End gateway portal that will take you to the floating outer islands of this space-like dimension. Grab your Ender pearls; it's time to go loot hunting!

OUTER ISLANDS

These islands can be visited only after you've defeated the Ender Dragon. They are generally more diverse than the End island; some are topped with chorus trees and some with End cities and ships. If the islands are close enough together – which they often are – you can travel between them using Ender pearls.

END CITY

End cities naturally generate on the outer islands, though they aren't always easy to find. They are unique because of their clusters of tall, purple structures, which can spawn as a single tower or many interconnected buildings. These are where you'll find valuable loot such as elytra.

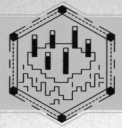

THE END:
TERRAIN

EXPLORING THE END

The End has much to offer in terms of valuable loot; however, large voids between islands and countless Endermen in every direction make the End a perilous dimension to explore. Here are some top tips for surviving it:

CHORUS FRUIT

This is the only source of food in the End, though it has a special effect. If you eat a chorus fruit, you'll be magically teleported to a nearby block. This can be annoying but also a life saver – especially if you've been hit by a shulker bullet (see shulkers on page 86). If you're floating away into space, eat one quickly to be brought back to land.

THREE-BLOCK-TALL ROOF

Endermen are roughly three blocks tall, meaning they can only fit in places that have at least three blocks of space! Build a platform above your head and stand under it to be safely out of their reach.

PUMPKIN HEAD

Staring into an Enderman's eyes makes them hostile – but not if you're wearing a pumpkin head! Pop one on and switch to third-person viewing mode so your sight isn't restricted.

The End terrain is unlike any other dimension. It is full of floating islands surrounded by a dark, hollow void. You can build bridges from island to island, but it'll require huge quantities of blocks. Thankfully, there is an easier way of traveling: Ender pearls.

An exit portal will activate upon defeating the Ender Dragon.

ENDER PEARL TRAVEL

Ender pearls are a way to travel in the End. When you throw one, you will be instantly teleported to wherever it lands; however, you will take fall damage and potentially spawn a pesky endermite. Simply aim high, throw the Ender pearl and keep your fingers crossed that your aim was true! Practicing in the Overworld before venturing into the End is recommended.

End stone cannot be moved by Endermen, making it the perfect bunker building material.

PEARL FARMING

You're going to need a LOT of pearls! The safest way to gather them is to create a pearl farm. To do this, build a bunker one block deep in the ground with a roof that is two blocks tall so the Endermen can't get in. When your bunker is ready, simply stare at as many Endermen as you can, then retreat into your bunker and attack them from below with your sword.

MOB ENCOUNTERS: THE END

ENDERMAN

Avoid eye contact with these tall, teleporting mobs – looking into their eyes will only provoke them!	♥	⚔
	40	7

Drops

ENDER DRAGON

This enormous dragon is fearsome in a battle and one of the hardest mobs to defeat.	♥	⛏	⚔
	200	6	10

Drops
●

SHULKER

This mob looks like an ordinary purpur block until it pops open and shoots bullets at you that make you levitate!	♥	⛏	🛡
	30	4	20

Drops

The End is full of powerful and strange hostile mobs, making it a place to be entered into with great caution. It is home to the fierce Ender Dragon as well as other mobs that will just as happily attack you. Make sure you're ready to take them all on! See page 47 for the mob icon key.

ENDERMITE

There's a chance that when you throw an Ender pearl, this short-lived little mob spawns to attack you.

♥	⚔
8	2

Drops

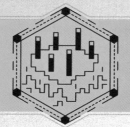

GENERATED STRUCTURES: THE NETHER & THE END

THE NETHER

NETHER FORTRESS

These towering Nether brick fortresses are found throughout the Nether dimension. Explorers will find Nether wart growing here – an essential brewing component – but also many dangerous mobs, including blazes.

BASTION REMNANT

Bastion remnants are decrepit buildings filled with piglins guarding valuable chests and treasure rooms. Explore these if you dare, but beware the wrath of the mighty piglin brutes!

Now that you've made it through the portals to the Nether and End, you're probably wondering what cool structures there are to explore and, more importantly, loot! Proceed with extra caution as these structures, though full of treasures, are guarded by some of Minecraft's fiercest mobs.

THE END

END CITIES

These purpur and End stone tower structures sprawl out into the dark sky. They are scattered around the End dimension and finding them can be time-consuming. However, their chests contain valuable loot, such as diamonds. Beware, though, as the treasure is protected by shulkers!

END SHIPS

Even rarer than the End cities are the End ships, which only generate in some of the End cities. If you do manage to find one, you're in luck, as you'll likely find a sought-after elytra on board. Elytras are your tickets to the skies!

EXIT PORTAL

Found on the main island, this portal is the only way back to the Overworld – besides dying, that is! It will return you to your respawn point and only works once a dragon egg has generated on top of it, after you've successfully defeated the Ender Dragon.

SPEEDY SETUP

BONUS CHEST

When you first set up your world, head to the More World Options menu and toggle Bonus Chest: On. This will generate a chest with useful basic items you can use early in the game to help speed up your process.

CAVE SHELTER

Not all homes need to look good and feel comfortable. For your first few nights, why not camp out in an existing cave? It won't have all the luxury of a handmade home, but it will certainly keep you safe from mobs.

SPEED FARMING

Farming doesn't have to take forever. Defeating skeletons will reward you with bones, which can be crafted into bone meal. These can then be used as a fertilizer to speed up the growth of crops, leaving you with a fully grown farm in no time!

Looking to make yourself at home in the Overworld as quickly as possible? If you're confident you have the skills to survive, you may be interested in skipping some game steps and rushing straight into mid game. You can shave hours off your early game with these neat tricks for experienced players.

TOOL RUSH

While it's good practice to create a full set of tools as soon as you can, it's not absolutely necessary. You can start with just a wooden pickaxe to gather cobblestone to create a cobblestone pickaxe. Then, immediately search for iron ore to craft a full set of iron tools, which will mine faster, hit harder and last longer.

1 Start with a wooden pickaxe to mine for stone.

2 A stone sword will keep you safe while you search for iron ore.

3 A full set of iron armor will reduce damage by 60%.

STRUCTURE RAIDING

Before you stop and set up camp, take a moment to explore and search for generated structures. These structures are packed with useful resources, from tools and equipment to food and blocks. Villages, for instance, are common across the Overworld and will provide you with food and seeds for farming. Just remember to be respectful of your friendly neighbors, or they won't welcome you back!

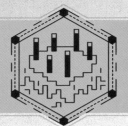

LATE-GAME CHALLENGES

THUNDERSTORMS

Just when you think you've learned everything there is to know about staying alive in Survival mode, a thunderstorm will come along to throw a wrench – or lightning – in the works! Though uncommon, thunderstorms can be very dangerous and maybe even deadly, with lightning striking down randomly, causing all kinds of havoc and setting you on fire if it hits you – sometimes twice! Pigs start turning into zombie piglins, villagers into witches, sea turtles start dropping bowls, and you may even find yourself suddenly surrounded by skeletal horsemen! Plan ahead and craft yourself some lightning rods from copper ingots to direct the lightning away from you and your flammable possessions.

You've now explored all the dimensions, but your journey doesn't have to end here. There's still plenty more content to enjoy, not to mention the game gets updated regularly with new mobs, blocks, items and biomes for you to discover. Here are just some of the challenges that still await you in Survival mode!

BEACONS

If you struggle to find your way back to base, a beacon might be just the thing for you. These bright beams of light can be seen for hundreds of blocks around in Java Edition, or up to 64 blocks in Bedrock Edition. But that's not all they're good for – beacons can also grant you various status effects while you're within range, such as Speed, Haste, Resistance, Jump Boost and Strength, making survival that much easier.

UNDERWATER

So you now know how to live on land, but what about in the ocean? Surviving underwater presents an obvious problem: breathing. It can also be incredibly dark below the depths. Luckily for us, there is a solution to both: a conduit. Building one of these in your underwater base will grant you Water Breathing, Night Vision and Haste status effects while you are within the conduit's range. It even attacks hostile mobs to keep your aquatic home safe from intruders! The sea is home to many creatures and treasures, so it's well worth exploring.

GOODBYE

Congratulations, you've journeyed to the end of the *Guide to Survival!* Are you feeling like a true adventurer? You should, because you've just learned the essentials of surviving in the Overworld, the Nether and the End.

But this is just the start. There's way more to learn and experience across the biomes of Minecraft. There's only so much we can squeeze into one book, after all!

So what's your next challenge? How about mounting an expedition into the depths of the sea? Or you could build yourself a beacon? Or what about digging way down into the deep dark?

Whatever comes next, we hope you remember that one of the biggest challenges we all face isn't about how skilled or experienced we are. It's about believing in yourself. If you can defeat that voice in your head that tries to tell you something is too hard, then you're already on the road to winning!

YOU CAN DO IT!

DISCOVER MORE MINECRAFT:
LEVEL UP YOUR GAME WITH THE OFFICIAL GUIDES

- ☐ *GUIDE TO COMBAT*
- ☐ *GUIDE TO CREATIVE*
- ☐ *GUIDE TO ENCHANTMENTS & POTIONS*
- ☐ *GUIDE TO FARMING*
- ☐ *GUIDE TO MINECRAFT DUNGEONS*

- ☐ *GUIDE TO OCEAN SURVIVAL*
- ☐ *GUIDE TO THE NETHER & THE END*
- ☐ *GUIDE TO PVP MINIGAMES*
- ☐ *GUIDE TO REDSTONE*
- ☐ *GUIDE TO SURVIVAL*

MORE MINECRAFT:

- ☐ *EPIC BASES*
- ☐ *EXPLODED BUILDS: MEDIEVAL FORTRESS*
- ☐ *LET'S BUILD! LAND OF ZOMBIES*
- ☐ *LET'S BUILD! THEME PARK ADVENTURE*
- ☐ *MAPS*

- ☐ *MINECRAFT FOR BEGINNERS*
- ☐ *MOBESTIARY*
- ☐ *THE SURVIVORS' BOOK OF SECRETS*
- ☐ *BLOCKOPEDIA*
- ☐ *BITE-SIZE BUILDS*
- ☐ *AMAZING BITE-SIZE BUILDS*

Penguin
Random
House